The Question & Answer Book

ROCKS & MINERALS

ROCKS & MINERALS

By Elizabeth Marcus
Illustrated by Dan Lawler

Troll Associates

Library of Congress Cataloging in Publication Data

Marcus, Elizabeth.
    Rocks and minerals.

    (The Question and answer book)
    Summary: Questions and answers provide basic information
about rocks and minerals, including their formation,
properties, and identification.
    1. Petrology—Juvenile literature.   2. Mineralogy—
Juvenile literature. [1. Petrology.   2. Mineralogy.
3. Questions and answers] I. Lawler, Dan, ill.
II. Title.   III. Series.
QE432.2.M27   1983   552   82-17424
ISBN 0-89375-876-0
ISBN 0-89375-877-9 (pbk.)

Copyright © 1983 by Troll Associates, Mahwah, New Jersey

Printed in the United States of America
10   9   8   7   6   5   4   3   2   1

When you hear the word "rock," what do you think of?

You might think of a huge boulder you'd like to climb. Or you might think of a tiny pebble you could throw into a lake to make ripples. But do you ever think of the whole Earth when you hear the word "rock"? You'd be right if you do, because our Earth is made mostly of rock.

There is rock under the soil, and even under the oceans. It goes all the way down through the center of the Earth.

Imagine that you could drill a hole to the center of the Earth. You would have to drill for almost 4,000 miles (6,400 kilometers) before you reached the center. All of that drilling would be through some form of rock. You would have to go through three layers, or zones, of rock.

What are the Earth's three layers of rock?

The outside layer is called the Earth's *crust*. The crust is about 20 miles (32 kilometers) thick under the land. Under the oceans, the crust is thinner—only about 5 miles (8 kilometers) thick.

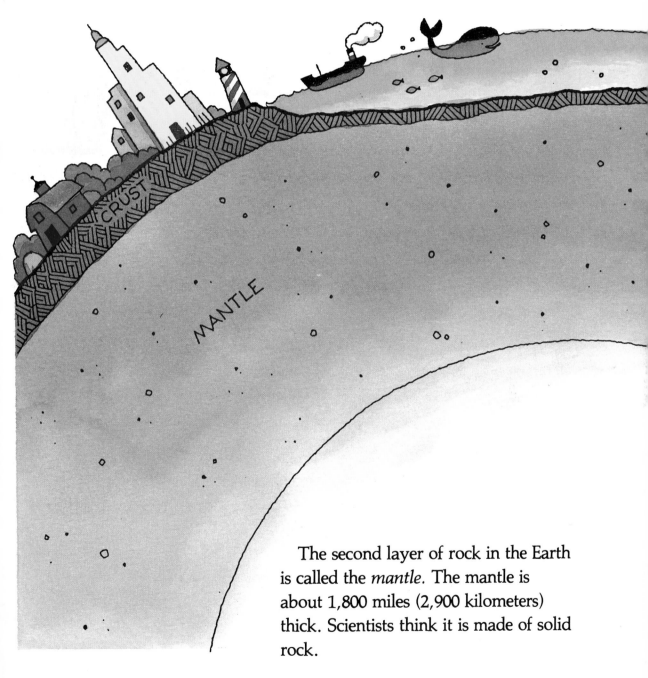

The second layer of rock in the Earth is called the *mantle*. The mantle is about 1,800 miles (2,900 kilometers) thick. Scientists think it is made of solid rock.

Finally, there is the Earth's *core*. At the very center of the core is the Earth's heaviest and hardest material. But the outer part of the core is hot. It is so hot that it is liquid! This is called *magma*, or melted rock.

You probably don't think of hot, liquid magma when you think about rocks. Instead, you probably think of cold, solid rocks. You might even have a collection of different kinds of rocks. If you don't already collect rocks, you might want to begin. A good way to start is to go for a nature walk.

Go on a rock hunt.

Walk along a brook or river, or along the edge of a seashore. Carry a bag with you, so you can bring back samples of interesting rocks. Collect as many different stones and rocks as you can find. Try to find rocks of different colors. Look for shiny rocks and rocks that are not so shiny. Search for smooth rocks and rocks that feel rough when you rub your fingers against them. Look for rocks that are hard and rocks that are soft.

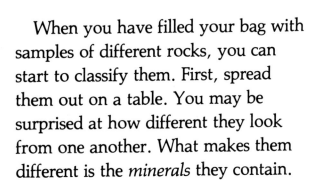

When you have filled your bag with samples of different rocks, you can start to classify them. First, spread them out on a table. You may be surprised at how different they look from one another. What makes them different is the *minerals* they contain.

What is a mineral?

A mineral is something in nature that is neither a plant nor an animal. Most rocks contain two or more minerals. To identify a mineral, you should look for four things.

First, look for *color*. Some minerals are light in color, while others are dark. They may be white, yellow, pink, red, blue, green, gray, or even black. But color is not always the best way to identify a mineral. This is because many minerals have extra chemicals in them that give them a different color than might be expected.

Second, look for *luster*, or shininess. Some minerals shine brightly, like metal. Others may look glassy or dull. Still others may have a pearly luster, like the inside of some seashells.

Third, look for *how the mineral breaks apart.* Some minerals split into thin, flat sheets. Some split into tiny cubes. Still others break up into pieces with different shapes.

Finally, look for *hardness.* You can test a mineral for hardness by trying to scratch it. Some minerals are so soft you can scratch them with your fingernail. Others can be scratched with a penny. Still others can be scratched with the steel blade of a penknife.

11

Can you identify these minerals?

Now that you know what to look for, you can try to identify some of the minerals in the rocks you collected.

One of the easiest minerals to identify is *mica*. It is often silvery-gray, and it sparkles. If you find a big flake of mica, dig at it carefully with a penknife. It should peel off in flat sheets that are thin enough for light to shine through. Mica is not very hard. You should be able to scratch it with your fingernail.

Most of the minerals you find will not be that soft. *Quartz* is a very hard mineral. It is also one of the most common minerals in the world. So you may be able to find some in one of your rock samples.

Look for a creamy-white or rose-colored stone. If it has a glassy luster, it may contain quartz. Scratch it with your fingernail. If you cannot make a mark, try scratching it with a penny.

Then scratch it with the blade of your penknife. If you still cannot make a mark, you can be almost sure this mineral is quartz.

The most common mineral in the world is called *feldspar.* Feldspar is always light in color. It is usually creamy white, light gray, or pink. It does not shine as much as mica or quartz, but it has a pearly luster. Feldspar is too hard to be scratched with a knife blade. But it is soft enough to be scratched with the sharp edge of a piece of quartz.

There is one sure way to tell if a mineral is feldspar. Wrap it in cloth, and break it with a hammer. A broken piece of feldspar will have little "steps" on its surface.

Another common mineral is called *calcite*. Calcite is a fairly soft mineral. You can scratch it easily with a knife blade. But this isn't a sure test. And you can't always tell calcite just by its color, either.

But there is one easy way to find out if a mineral is calcite. Sprinkle a few drops of vinegar on it, and watch what happens. Vinegar is a weak acid. It dissolves calcite and makes it "fizz." Do you see tiny bubbles forming? If so, you can be sure you have a sample of calcite.

There are many other kinds of
minerals. But now that you know how
to recognize mica, quartz, feldspar,
and calcite, you are ready to identify
some of the rocks in your collection.

Can you identify these rocks?

One of the easiest rocks to identify is *granite*. Granite
may be gray or pink, and is sprinkled with specks of black
and white, like pepper and salt. Feldspar is the mineral that
gives granite its gray or pink color. There is a lot of
feldspar in granite.

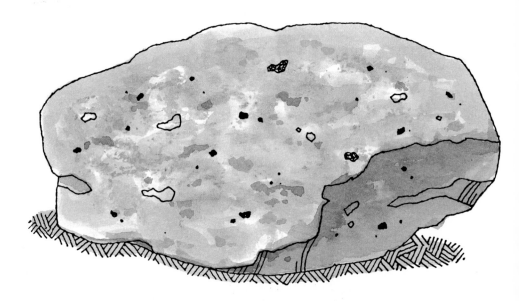

Other minerals in granite include mica and quartz. If you
look closely, you should be able to see shiny bits of mica,
and tiny pieces of light-colored quartz. Usually all the
mineral grains in granite are very small, and about the
same size.

You probably have some reddish or brown chunks of rock in your collection. Put a newspaper under two of them, and scrape them together. If tiny grains of sand break off, you probably have a rock called *sandstone*.

Sandstone is made mostly of quartz and sand, cemented together with calcite. Small amounts of other minerals give sandstone its color. It is usually brown or red, but sometimes it is gray or yellowish in color.

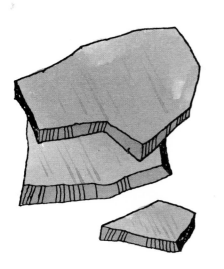

Now look for a flat, gray rock in your collection. Is it made up of different layers? Is it so soft that you can scratch it with a penny? If so, it may be *shale*. To find out for sure, spill some water on it. When shale is wet, it smells like damp earth. Although it is usually gray, shale can also be red or brown.

Another common rock is *limestone*. Limestone is usually gray or white. It is made almost entirely of calcite. This means that a weak acid, like vinegar, will dissolve it.

When rainwater mixes with a gas in the air, it makes a weak acid. The acid dissolves or washes away the soft calcite that is in limestone deposits. This leaves hollowed-out holes or caves. That's why many limestone deposits contain underground caves. Some caves contain strange rock formations called stalagmites and stalactites. These rocks look like long icicles. They hang from the ceilings of caves or rise from the ground. These unusual rocks are made of calcite that was dissolved in water. As the water dried up, the calcite was left in strange new formations.

How are rocks formed?

Limestone, sandstone, shale, and granite are rocks that are easy to find and easy to identify. But there are many other kinds of rocks, too. Where do they all come from? How are different kinds of rocks formed?

Scientists divide most rocks into three groups, according to how the rocks were formed. Some are called *igneous* rocks. Others are called *metamorphic* rocks. Still others are called *sedimentary* rocks.

What are igneous rocks?

The word *igneous* means "fiery." Igneous rocks had a fiery beginning. If you could watch a volcano erupt, you would be watching igneous rocks being formed. The lava that flows from a volcano is hot magma, or liquid rock. It is being pushed up from deep inside the Earth. When it reaches the surface, it cools rapidly, and turns into igneous rock. Basalt and obsidian are two kinds of igneous rock that are formed this way.

Igneous rock is sometimes formed just below the surface of the Earth. When hot magma cannot break through the surface, it cools more slowly. When it cools enough to harden, it turns to solid rock. Granite is a kind of igneous rock that is formed this way.

What are metamorphic rocks?

Metamorphic rocks are formed differently. *Metamorphic* means "changed." Pressure, heat, or strong chemicals can change other kinds of rocks into metamorphic rocks. Unless you are an expert, it is usually hard to recognize metamorphic rocks. They may have once been igneous rocks, or they may have once been another kind of rock, called sedimentary rock. Slate and marble are two kinds of metamorphic rock.

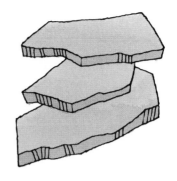

What are sedimentary rocks?

Sedimentary rocks are formed differently from igneous or metamorphic rocks. They are formed from sediment, or material that collects for millions of years. Dirt, sand, bits of rock, and other materials are washed into valleys or into the sea. There, they pile up in layers. Over long periods of time, the layers of sediment become sedimentary rock.

Sandstone is one type of sedimentary rock. Shale is another. Shale is made from muddy sediment. That's why it smells like damp earth when it is wet.

Limestone is another type of sedimentary rock. It was formed from the broken shells of countless tiny sea animals. When these animals died, their shells settled on the floor of the ocean. Over millions of years, the layers of shells turned into rock.

Then great pressures within the Earth forced parts of the ocean's floor to rise up. Mountains were formed, and the sea drained away. That's why limestone formations can now be found in places that are far from the ocean, and far above sea level.

Look carefully at a piece of limestone, shale, or sandstone. You will
probably see bands of different shades
in the rock. These are the different
layers of sediment that were piled on
top of one another long ago.

Sedimentary rocks have a story to tell.

The story is in the layers of the rocks and in the fossils
the rocks may contain. Fossils are traces of ancient plants
and animals. A fossil can be a shell, a bone, or a skeleton
that has been turned into rock. It can also be a footprint in
a rock—or the imprint of an entire animal or plant.

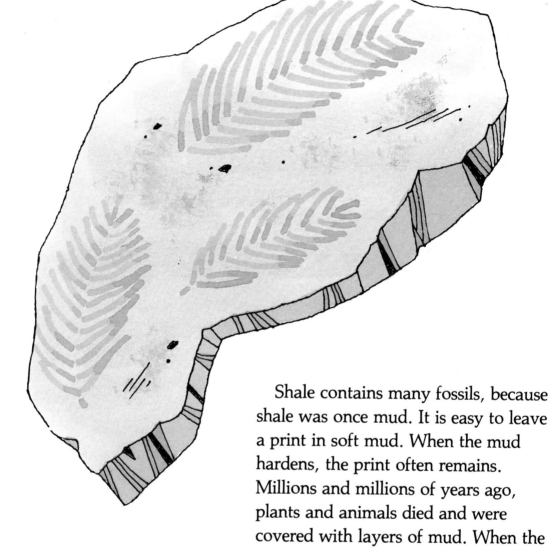

Shale contains many fossils, because shale was once mud. It is easy to leave a print in soft mud. When the mud hardens, the print often remains. Millions and millions of years ago, plants and animals died and were covered with layers of mud. When the muddy sediment turned to rock, the exact shape of the plant or animal was often preserved.

What kinds of plants and animals lived millions of years ago? What was the weather like? How were parts of the Earth formed? How has the Earth changed? Rocks and fossils can help scientists to answer these questions.

Secrets of the past

Geologists are scientists who study the Earth and its rocks. Paleontologists are scientists who study fossils. Geologists and paleontologists can learn the secrets of the past by studying rocks and fossils.

You may be lucky enough to find a fossil of a plant or animal in a piece of shale. But even if your rock collection doesn't have any fossils, you can see them in a museum. Many museums have fascinating displays of fossils, as well as fine collections of many different rocks and minerals.

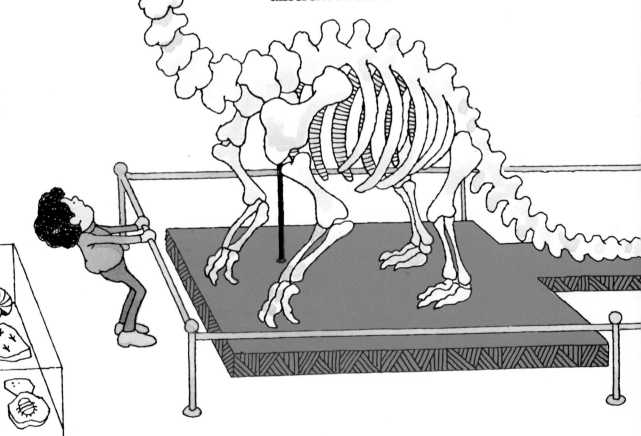

How do we use rocks?

Sedimentary rocks do more than hold the records of the past. They are used in the present—in many ways. Limestone is one of the most useful sedimentary rocks. Crushed limestone is used in cement and concrete. Powdered limestone is used in plaster. Sandstone—another sedimentary rock—is also used for building. Have you ever heard of a brownstone house? The "brownstone" is really sandstone.

Igneous and metamorphic rocks are also used for building. Granite—an igneous rock—is beautiful and very hard. When it is polished, it shines like a mirror. You may have seen it in the lobbies of such buildings as banks and courthouses. Slate—a metamorphic rock—breaks into thin, flat pieces. The tiles on the roofs of some houses are made of slate. And marble—another metamorphic rock—is often used for monuments and statues.

All the rocks that are used for building come from *quarries*. A quarry is a big open pit in the earth. The rocks are blasted apart and lifted out of the quarry by cranes.

How do we use minerals?

The minerals in rocks have many uses, too. Did you know that salt is a mineral? In very cold weather, rock salt is often used to help keep water from freezing on sidewalks. You probably use table salt every day. Graphite is another mineral you use every day. When you write with a pencil, you are writing with a stick of graphite.

Minerals that are metals are especially useful. Think of all the things around you that have iron, copper, tin, silver, aluminum, or lead in them. Each of these metals comes from *ore*. Ore is rock that has useful metals in it. But to be called ore, rock must contain enough metal to be economically taken out and used.

Ore is dug out of mines. Some mines are deep under the ground. Some are near the surface of the ground. Surface mines are called open-pit mines, or strip mines. In these kinds of mines, great chunks of ore are blasted or dug out of the earth.

How to learn more about rocks

Geologists help mining companies decide where to start new mines. They begin by learning all they can about the rocks and minerals in the area. You may not be a geologist, but you can learn about the rocks and minerals in your area. A good place to start is with the samples you collected on your nature walk.

You can use egg cartons to keep your samples of rocks and minerals separated from one another. Make sure you label each sample as you identify it. You should also write down where and when you found each one.

Rocks are all around you. So it shouldn't be hard to add to your collection. There are many interesting rocks near streams or by the seashore. Look in your garden, in your back yard, in empty lots, and in fields.

You don't have to collect all the rocks you see. You can learn a lot simply by looking at rocks—in the park, or on a trip to a quarry, for example. If you live in a city, look through the hole in the fence around a building excavation. From this safe place you may be able to see different layers of earth, and many different kinds of rock.

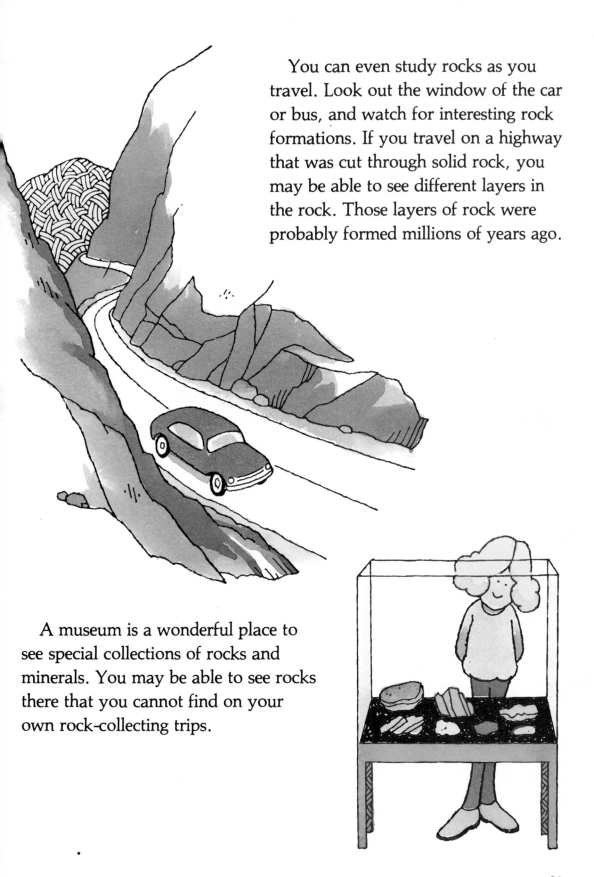

You can even study rocks as you travel. Look out the window of the car or bus, and watch for interesting rock formations. If you travel on a highway that was cut through solid rock, you may be able to see different layers in the rock. Those layers of rock were probably formed millions of years ago.

A museum is a wonderful place to see special collections of rocks and minerals. You may be able to see rocks there that you cannot find on your own rock-collecting trips.

As a rock collector, you may even want to trade and exchange your rocks with someone who has rocks you can't find. Then you'll be on your way to becoming a real "rock hound"—a collector of all kinds of rocks and minerals.